This is
the gripping, true story
of Mrs. Morag McDougall,
nearly dead from a series
of debilitating heart attacks,
and her amazing healing
at a Los Angeles Kathryn Kuhlman
meeting.

10,000 Miles For A Miracle

Kathryn Kuhlman

10,000 Miles For A Miracle

DIMENSION BOOKS
BETHANY FELLOWSHIP, INC.
Minneapolis, Minnesota

DIMENSION BOOKS
are published by Bethany Fellowship,
Inc., 6820 Auto Club Road, Minneapolis,
Minnesota 55438

Printed in U.S.A.

Contents

Introduction

All the way from the "land down under"—on a wing and a prayer, so to speak—Mrs. Morag McDougall came ten thousand miles for a miracle.

Born and reared in Australia, Mrs. McDougall is the wife of a prominent oil industry executive in Melbourne. Her husband, Jack, was purchasing manager for British Petroleum in Australia for twenty years and served a term as national president of the Institute of Purchasing and Supply Management. He was also chairman of the Oil Companies Materials Committee for ten years.

He is now the executive officer of the Australian American Association.

Nearly dead from a series of debilitating heart attacks, Mrs. McDougall had just about given up hope when she happened to hear of the Miracle Services conducted by Kathryn Kuhlman.

"If Miss Kuhlman would come even as close as California," she told her friend in Melbourne, "I would jump a plane."

"But don't you know," her friend exclaimed, "Kathryn Kuhlman has meetings once a month in Los Angeles!"

Ten days later, Morag and her son Bruce were winging their way toward America—expecting a miracle.

As in the days when Jesus walked the dusty roads of Galilee, healing all those who came to Him, so He still reaches out and touches those who come to Him in simple faith. The story of Morag McDougall's healing is surely one of the most tender and exciting stories of the decade.

1. That Fainting Spell

My housecoat around me, I cracked the front door and peered at the early morning mist. Behind me, Jack, dressed in his usual conservative brown business suit, gently wrapped his arms around my waist. I loved the feel of his freshly shaved cheek against the side of my neck. He was ready for his day at the office.

Moving around me and out the door, he brushed his lips across mine. "See you at dinner, dear," he smiled. "And happy anniversary."

Fifteen years of marriage to the busiest, yet most wonderful man in all Australia, I thought. I leaned against the doorsill and followed him with my eyes as he moved briskly down the walk toward the driveway. The light fog hung in the tops of the eucalyptus trees. The gray-green trees symbolized Australia—casual, almost graceless, slightly eccentric, robust in temperament. They scattered their bark on the parched soil of the outback in the remote interior of our rugged continent, and dropped their leaves in our garden in times of drought. Like the maple tree of Canada, they represented all that is uniquely Australian.

Jack was like that, I thought, as I watched him get in his car and pull into the street of Ascot Vale on his way to work. Still a young man, he occupied a most important position in the petroleum business on the continent. Even so, his vigorous drive was combined with a deep faith in God. Despite the grief we had suffered when our blind child had died, and despite our son Bruce's affliction, some of which could have been caused by brain damage, these had been fifteen years of happiness. I was a blessed woman.

Jack's car disappeared down the street, but I lingered at the door. A skylark had risen from a nearby paddock and was lifting his voice in magnificent song, heralding the coming of the day. The rays of the early morning sun, filtering through the ground fog, reflected in the dewdrops on the rose bushes beside the house. And overhead, the gray sky, just moments before sparkling with the stars of the Southern Cross, was now turning a soft pink. Then, almost as if an unseen conductor had waved his baton, the gum trees were filled with a symphony of sound as the birds came alive and stretched their voices toward God—a soft serenade of dawn.

There was a scent of spring in the air. It was September in Australia and before long the summer winds would blow and the people of Melbourne would shed their jackets and head for the beaches and tennis courts. But this morning, as the sky turned from rose to pale yellow and then light blue, everything was springtime.

The words of Browning's Pippa, learned in school when I was a mere child, danced through my mind:

> The year's at the spring
> And day's at the morn'
> Morning's at seven;
> The hillside's dew-pearled;
> The lark's on the wing;
> The snail's on the thorn:
> God's in His heaven—
> All's right with the world.

God was in His heaven—of that I was sure. My parents had both died when I was young and I had been reared on a farm in rural Victoria. Through it all, moving from aunts to uncles, I was aware of His hand. Then the year before I married Jack, I met God personally— through Jesus Christ. Yes, God was in His heaven.

But deep inside, like a cloud passing the sun, there was an uneasiness. All was not right with the world—at least with *my* world. Perhaps it had to do with that fainting spell Wednesday as we were on our way to church. I had never felt that way before. It was as though my veins had simply squeezed tight and all the blood that normally surged through my system disappeared. In that brief instant, I had the sensation of dying. The men carried me to the church but I was soon on my feet again. Then there was Jack's worried look after it was all over as he insisted I see a doctor.

I tried to put him off; yet, when something goes wrong in your body, what other option is there but to go to a doctor. *If Jesus were still on earth*, I often thought, *I would go to Him*. After all, the Bible said He healed all those who came to Him. But Jesus was not here. He was in heaven and, it seemed, we were left alone on earth to struggle along the best we could.

2. "You Have Had A Heart Seizure"

The sound of the boys' voices brought me back to the present. Rob was eight—the picture of good health. Bruce, in his thirteenth year, was one of those special children that had to struggle all the time just to keep up: those horrible seizures since he was three. And then the day when he was playing under the baby's pram—back when little blind Johnny was still alive. The doctor had put Bruce in eyeglasses shortly before, and still unaccustomed to them, he had raised up and smashed the glass into his eye. When

I got to him he was crying and rubbing his eye with his fist, grinding the slivers of glass deeper and deeper into the eyeball. The doctors wanted to remove the eye, but I insisted God would perfect him also. They left it, though he was totally blind in that eye.

But no time to reminisce. The day was upon me. Get the boys off to school, then visit the doctor. "God's in His heaven and that's *dinkum*,"* I said to no one in particular, and started down the hall to the boys' room.

The boys off to school, I started straightening up around the house. Why did I tire so easily? Why this nagging feeling that something was wrong? I was taking the last of the breakfast dishes off the kitchen table and wiping the counter with a damp towel when I became aware of a strange sensation in my left arm. Heat. That's what it was. A spreading warmth from my shoulder to my fingertips. *Odd*, I thought. But I finished with the kitchen and started down the

---

* Australian phrase for "real," or "true."

hall when the tingling suddenly changed into fire. Searing! Burning! I gasped in agony as scorching pain ran the length of my arm. I tried to move my hand, but the arm was powerless, paralyzed, hanging at my side with liquid fire.

"Dear God!" I choked out as I stumbled into the bedroom. "Oh please . . . ," and I fell across the still unmade bed. Nothing, not childbirth nor the kidney infection, matched the pain I was now experiencing.

Gradually it subsided and strangely enough, I dozed off. When I awoke, moments later, the sun was streaming through the big bay window in the bedroom. Tiny dust particles, like elves on a golden staircase, were dancing up and down the sunbeam. Had it been a dream? I sat up in bed, rubbing my eyes and smoothing my hair. Had I imagined the whole thing? No, there was still the faint hint of a tingling sensation in my left arm.

"Think, old girl," I said aloud. "Try to remember what happened." But I could not. My mind simply blocked out the ordeal as though it had never taken place.

I finished my housework and walked two blocks to the tram. Melbourne is the second largest city in Australia, and our suburb of Ascot Vale is one of the many smaller communities that surround it. It was a short train ride into the city.

My first stop was the clinic where several doctors had their offices. After a quick examination the young doctor said, "Just nerves, nothing to be alarmed about."

"Sorry," I argued, "but my husband insisted I see a specialist."

"But that can't be arranged for two weeks," the doctor replied.

"Then I'll be back in two weeks," I said. "If I live that long," I added, chuckling.

I had meant it as a joke. But as I turned to leave the clinic, I had to fight off a dark foreboding that my words bordered on being prophetic.

Back home that afternoon I went through the motions of preparing the evening meal. Since the war beef was plentiful in Australia, and Jack's gentle hug as he came in and smelled roast was all the reward I needed.

At dinner Jack surveyed the table, then looked up at me. "Like cheese and wine, you improve with age, Morag," he said with a sly grin.

"Wine I know nothing about, thank you," I laughed. "But since I'm approaching forty I'll identify with cheese."

Jack reached over and squeezed my hand, then bowed his head and asked grace. "Lord, I thank you for these fifteen years . . . may we have many more . . ."

My mind wandered as he finished his prayer. Was fifteen years with Jack all I would have? Rob could grow up and take care of himself, but who would care for Bruce if I were gone? I tried to enjoy the dinner, but fingers of fear had snatched my appetite.

The boys were up from the table, leaving Jack and me alone for a few moments. He was in a hurry to attend a Sunday School teachers' meeting at Flemington Presbyterian Church that night, but I needed to talk. I reached over and touched his hand.

"Jack, this morning . . . the strangest thing . . . " He listened as I described the pain.

"You had better go down to the doctor in the morning," he said.

"I was there this morning," I told him. "He said it was just nerves. I have to wait two weeks to see the specialist."

"Then I want you to go back in the morning and tell them it's not nerves. Something must be wrong."

Jack was on his feet, reaching for his coat. "It was a good dinner," he said. "And you are a good wife. I want to keep you around for a long time, so just take it easy tonight. I'll be home early."

The children were in bed when it returned. Like a dark intruder it came into our home. There was nowhere to hide as it sank its ugly talons into my body. It started the same way as before—tingling, then warmth, then searing pain in my arm, spreading across my neck and into my chest.

Surely, Jack will be home soon, I kept

thinking. But the minutes dragged into centuries as the pain raged through the top half of my body. I couldn't even cry out for the boys. Was this the end? Would Jack return and find me on the bed, limp in death?

I looked up and saw Jack standing in the door of the bedroom. His face paled as he saw me twisting on the bed, my head drenched in perspiration. Without a word he grabbed the phone and called the clinic. A young doctor, a locum*, was on duty. By the time he had reached the house I was fighting for each breath. The doctor gave me an injection, checked my heart and took my blood pressure. He then motioned for Jack to follow him into the other room.

I could hear Jack's voice in the hall-way outside the room. "Don't tell me that . . . she was at your clinic this morning . . . you said nothing serious . . ."

There was more talk, but things were becoming fuzzy as the sedative took hold. When they returned Jack bent over me.

---

* A resident doctor.

His eyes were red and swollen. *That's funny*, I thought, *Jack crying? I must be worse than I think.*

"Your husband tells me you are a very sensible person," the young doctor said.

I tried to grin through the pain. "Well, that's not what he tells me."

The doctor smiled slightly and placed his stethoscope against the upper part of my chest. "You have had a heart seizure, Mrs. McDougall. We are going to get you to the hospital and do everything we can for you. But I do not want you to move a muscle until the ambulance arrives."

3. Public Opinion Was More Important Than Healing

I was in and out of consciousness by the time the ambulance pulled into the driveway. Vaguely, as through a foggy glass, I could see the boys' faces peering from their bedroom window—the fright in their eyes reflecting in the eerie red glow of the flashing light on the ambulance. Then the doors shut behind me and I slipped into blackness. I knew that just beyond that misty shadow was the silhouette of death—so close I could almost reach out and take his hand. How easy it would be to go with him. But if

I did, who would care for Bruce? . . . I hung on, determined to live.

I was six weeks in the Royal Melbourne Hospital. Dr. Maurice Etheridge, who was to become a dear friend over the years ahead, was my heart specialist. He explained I had barely escaped death during a coronary occlusion—a clot to the heart.

"You've cleared a big hurdle," he said when he dismissed me. "You came as close to dying, yet living, as anyone I've ever known."

I was alive, and although I left the hospital with what the doctor called an "enlarged heart," I was able to return home and resume a partial routine. The doctor assured me, however, that I would always be on medication, that I could never again exert myself physically, and that the condition could return any time—with even more serious results. Although I didn't ask, I knew what he meant by that. I could drop dead at any moment.

The next three months were spent recuperating at home. We had a nurse, which helped. Then in February I was given another chance. Despite the fact that Jack and I had been officers in our Presbyterian church, we were interested when a well-known American evangelist came to Melbourne proclaiming that miracles and healing were for today.

"Do you think we could attend some of the meetings?" I asked Jack, realizing they were being held in a tent.

Jack grinned. "Your parents may have been Scottish, Mrs. McDougall, but you're an Aussie to the bone. We'll go tonight."

It was my first introduction to spiritual healing. Even though I did not understand all the evangelist's methods, there was no denying that God was at work—and that people were being healed. We went back again a second time. During the service, when the evangelist announced that the Holy Spirit was just as powerful today as He was at Pentecost, I felt something happen in my body. It wasn't much, just a sensation—more like a tingle, I guess. I thought very little about it until two days later when I was downtown in a department store buying something for the boys. Ever since my first attack, more than three years before, I had been unable to walk up stairs. I always took the elevator. But this morning, since I was in a hurry to make my purchase and then get on to the doctor for my regular checkup, I forgot. Instead of taking the elevator, I bounded up the stairs. It wasn't until I reached the top that I realized I could breathe. For three years I had been able to breathe only in short gasps. Now, even though my heart was fluttering from the exertion of climbing the stairs, I could breathe deeply.

Amazed, I hurried on to the doctor's office. Had God healed me? Was the sensation I had felt the other night really the Holy Spirit? Dr. Etheridge checked me out and then took an X-ray.

"This is absolutely amazing," he said, as he held the negative up to the light. "Your heart has returned to its normal size. It is no longer enlarged. Tell me what has happened to you."

I bit my lips. I wanted, desperately, to testify of the healing power of God, but I was afraid to tell Dr. Etheridge that I had been to the meetings—and that God had touched me. So I said nothing. Like Simon Peter of old, I refused to testify that I had been touched by God.

Even as I left the doctor's office I felt I could sense the sad eyes of Jesus on me. The healing was mine. He had given it to me. But I had refused to take it . . . had refused to testify.

Exhausted, I had to retire early that night. Public opinion was more important than healing. Whatever I had received from God I no longer had. Standing in my bedroom, looking out the bay windows at the eucalyptus trees in the front yard, I thought of the recent decision on the part of several Australian cities to cut down the gray-green eucalyptus and replace them with more decorous trees imported from overseas. It was almost as if the cities were like me— ashamed of God's gift. I crawled into bed, too tired to cry.

For two years I struggled, vainly, to regain my former strength. Nothing seemed to help. Sometimes there would be weeks which passed when I couldn't even get outside of the house. Gradually, though, as I read my Bible, I discovered that although it is God's intent for a person to get old and die, nowhere does it seem to be God's intent for people to get sick and die—especially to linger on with a debilitating disease. Yet I was getting sicker and sicker.

Healing, as I came to understand it in the Bible, was not so much an event as it was a state in which a person lives. The Christian, it seemed, should be continually healed of all his diseases. After all, didn't the Bible say of Jesus, "By his stripes we *are* healed"? I yearned to walk in that kind of health. Instead, bit by bit, I was dying.

Even while I was pondering all this in my heart, I had another serious attack. I had been in bed most of the day with a throbbing headache. Towards evening I had arisen to fix the dinner meal for the family. Rob, who was eleven by then, had been home all day with a cold. By dinner time, however, he was feeling better and joined the rest of us at the little table in the kitchen.

Winters in Melbourne, which last from June until September, are usually rather mild. However, I had been cold all day and by dinner was actually shivering. Jack had pulled a small radiator (heater) up close to my chair at the kitchen table when suddenly I began to feel great flashes of heat through my body. I tried to speak, but nothing came out. I knew my mouth was moving, but I heard no words. I raised my hand to motion Jack to move the radiator away from my chair, but when I did I felt myself falling.

Everything went into slow motion. I could see Jack rising out of his chair, could see the look of panic on his face. I saw the terrified look on Bruce's face and the tears appearing in Rob's eyes —all as I fell toward the floor. Then there was pain—pounding, pulsating, stabbing through my head. I knew I was having a stroke.

Jack was at my side almost the moment I hit the floor. The children were terrified. It was as though that hideous, foreign monster had invaded our home again, bent on carrying me off.

I tried to speak, to ask Jack to call

the doctor. But instead of words, all I heard coming from my lips were slurred, animal-like sounds. My right side was dead—no feeling. Jack tried to help me into a sitting position but I could not move my right arm or leg; it was as if they belonged to somebody else. Rob and Bruce half-carried, half-dragged me to the couch. I could not get my eyes off my right arm. How strange it looked, dangling there by my side. I reached over with my left hand and grabbed the wrist, pulling my arm up onto the couch beside me. It was like holding somebody else's hand. There was no feeling, no sensation whatever.

I could hear Jack in the kitchen, dialing the phone. The first doctor said he could not possibly come; he had a clinic full of people. Another doctor was on his way to a hospital emergency. Jack finally reached the specialist, Dr. Etheridge, who agreed to come at once. By that time the first effects of the stroke had subsided, and I could feel some sensation returning to my arm and leg.

Dr. Etheridge examined me, called it

a "spasm," then gave me an injection and some medicine. He first insisted I go to the hospital, but when I objected he allowed me to stay home, providing I would remain bedfast for at least ten days.

4. "We Must Do Something Further"

The effects of the stroke wore off, but my heart condition grew progressively worse. Over the next fifteen years I became a semi-invalid, in and out of the hospital, often confined to the bed for days at a time.

However, there were some good things that happened in those years. One of them was meeting David and Olive Reekie. David was unlike any other Christian I had ever met. Most of the people in Australia are church people, although many of them are simply

C & E (Christmas and Easter) Christians. But the Reekies' brand of Christianity was different from most of our friends . They talked to God as if they knew Him personally. Christianity was more than a Sunday religion for them. When I quizzed them about their intimate relationship with the Lord, they said it was because they had been "filled with the Holy Spirit."

I remembered the term. It had been used by the American evangelist. I had, of course, heard of the Holy Spirit. He was the Third Person of the Trinity. We sang about Him in our Presbyterian church—"Praise Father, Son, and Holy Ghost." And in the Apostles' Creed, which we so routinely droned each Communion Sunday morning, there was a line which said, "I believe in the Holy Ghost." However, I didn't know any more about "the Holy Ghost" than I knew about the "holy catholic church." They were just words—words and phrases. Empty. Meaningless.

The filling of the Holy Spirit was not meaningless to the Reekies, however.

Nor were the gifts of the Spirit. They believed in healing—and in miracles. Many times when I grew faint in the night, when my heartbeat slowed and my legs crumpled under me, or when the pain surged through my chest and down my arm, Jack would rush to the phone to call the Reekies, even before he called the doctor. Countless times David and Olive got out of bed in the middle of the night and rushed to my house to pray for me. And countless times God answered their prayers. Yet healing, final healing, was always just beyond my fingertips of prayer.

Rob grew tall—above six feet—and married. He had completed his degree at the university and had been a good football and cricket player. All that I lacked in my own life, all that Bruce lacked in his, seemed to be made up for in Rob. When his wife, Susan, presented him with a wee lassie named Caitlin, it was one of the happiest days of my life.

"You must not lean so much on Rob," Jack told me one evening. "I, too, am proud of his accomplishments. But our faith must be in the Lord. It is upon Him we must lean and look for our satisfaction—not in the accomplishments of our son."

I laughed. "I am not leaning on Rob. I'm simply proud of him, that's all."

"But what if he were taken from us?" Jack probed.

"Then I would feel as if my very life would be gone," I said.

Yet Rob is strong and healthy. What could possibly happen to him?

The thought haunted me. Was God preparing me for something? Or was it simply my own negative attitude which had begun to look for everything to go wrong?

I had little time to think about it, for something else happened in my life, an experience which was to be the beginning of an entire new dimension of living. David and Olive Reekie were attending a small Full Gospel church in Melbourne. They invited us to go with them to one of the Sunday night meetings. I had a growing desire to walk in health and happiness the way the Reekies walked in it, and Jack and I both readily accepted their invitation.

At the close of the service that night the pastor, Mr. Braley, stepped out from behind the pulpit and spoke informally to the congregation. He said, "Is there someone here with a special need? Perhaps you'd like to be born again and become a Christian. Or, if you are already a Christian but lack the power in your life, perhaps you'd like to receive the fullness of the Holy Spirit. If so, you may come to the altar and we'll pray for you."

I turned to Jack. "I'm going up," I said with determination that shocked even me. "I want this baptism of the Holy Spirit that David and Olive have. If this will help me in my Christian walk, if this will help me pray better—then I want it."

Jack looked at me intently as I spoke. I saw his eyes filling with tears. He nodded. "I think we've waited long enough. We'll go together."

We stood, side by side, holding hands at the altar. The pastor and David Reekie laid their hands on us. "Lord, fill them with Your Holy Spirit," they prayed.

Yet nothing happened. At least, I didn't feel anything happen. The minister finished praying and I looked up, shaking my head. "I guess I'm just one of those stubborn Presbyterians," I said.

There was nothing else to do but return home.

Before going to bed we sat quietly in the living room. There was so much I did not understand. I loved the Lord. Jack and I, Rob and Bruce, we all loved the Lord. We were followers of Jesus Christ. Yet our lives seemed spiritually powerless and my body was dying. I knew there was more to Christianity than I had experienced. I saw it in the lives of people like the Reekies. Was it not for me too?

I was weary and rested my head as I began to pray. Softly, barely murmuring my conversation of praise, I prayed, unaware of time and space, unaware that Jack had left his chair and was hovering over me. Jack told me later, much later, that he was afraid to touch me, for the glory of God was all around me. Yet to me it all seemed so natural.

I do not know how long all this lasted, but I do know that as I rested in my chair, my lips now silent, I felt peace.

In Australia the interior of the continent is referred to as the "outback." There is very little vegetation and the ranches, or stations as we call them, must cover vast areas of land to provide enough grass for the sheep and cattle. Beyond the outback is the "back-of-beyond." It is here, in this wilderness region of rugged mountain ranges, arid wastelands and sun-bleached deserts, that the roads run out and quit. One hundred years ago a group of rugged explorers, tramping their way through the MacDonnell range of mountains, stumbled across a spring—a sort of oasis—lying almost in the center of the continent, a thousand miles from Adelaide on the south and Darwin on the North. Alice Springs lies in the very midst of the back-of-beyond, yet it is the center of a pastoral region that extends outward almost one hundred miles—springs in the desert.

I had been living my spiritual life in the back-of-beyond, perishing for lack of moisture. Now, in the quietness of my own living room, there had begun to flow out of me streams of living water, bringing life to the parched wasteland of my soul.

I drank deeply, and for the first time in years, found myself believing there was more to come.

But I was not yet out of the desert. In the late fall, just before Easter, I returned to the hospital. Many times during that summer, I had wakened at night to find my heart beating wildly as though it were trying to force blood through a closed passage. On at least two occasions, when I was hanging out clothes during the hot months of January and February, my legs buckled under me as my tired heart seemed to quit. On these occasions I would have to go back to bed for a week or more, and twice the doctor put me in the hospital for observation. My blood pressure soared and dipped—to dangerous extremes—and I realized my condition was rapidly deteriorating. Dr. Etheridge finally insisted I return to the hospital for treatment. "We must do something further," he said.

5. "Surely You Don't Want Him Now"

Doctors at the Royal Melbourne Hospital put me through a new series of tests. Among these was a strange examination where the doctors attached wires to my body which led to some sort of television screen. I gave them reports as they pushed buttons. It took a fair while and the next day Dr. Etheridge came into my room to make his report.

The aorta valve, he said, was narrowed down until only a small amount of blood could pass through. "It is like a pipe that has formed a crust on the inside. It must be replaced immediately."

"Are you suggesting an operation?" I asked.

"Not suggesting," he said soberly. "I am telling you it is imperative."

"Will the operation cure me?" I asked.

"We don't know," he said, pacing the room at the end of my bed. "We might open you and then have to sew you right back up again. It might be that the tissue has been irreparably torn. At best, it is risky business."

"Look," I said, "I think Jack and I should pray about this."

Dr. Etheridge nodded. "Of course," he said. "But you must not wait long. You are critically ill and any sudden shock could kill you."

Neither Jack nor I felt God wanted me to have the operation, so we trusted that there would be no sudden shock to force me back into the hospital.

We were wrong. Within weeks from the time I left the hospital my very soul was wrenched from me. Rob died! My son, the pride of my life, the father of my precious granddaughter—dead. There

44

was no warning. He was the picture of health. The typical young Australian, strong, muscular, tall and handsome as they come. One day he was with us, the next he was gone.

We had driven to Adelaide, in South Australia, for a few days. Susan, Rob's wife, was down there on a visit and we had brought little Caitlin down. As we drove through the city I sensed something was wrong, like a dark presence in the car. Rob was quiet—too quiet. Somehow, in the inner places where only mothers know, I sensed all was not right.

"Rob, are you not feeling well?" I asked casually.

He glanced at me from the corner of his eye. I knew he did not want to alarm me because of my health. "I'm all right, Mum," he said. "Just a bit of dizziness."

Yet I could tell it was more than that —far more. His head was twitching and the beads of perspiration stood out on

Picture on next two pages showing Kathryn Kuhlman before an audience at the Sacramento Memorial Auditorium, Sacramento, California.

his face like dew on the morning grass.

"Pull over to the left, dear, and stop,"
I said.

Adelaide is a beautiful city, a city of
churches, parks and gardens. Rob was
having difficulty, but he steered the car
to the curb near one of these small parks.
He reached for the ignition key, but collapsed over the steering wheel. Near
panic, I grabbed him by the shoulders
and pulled him back in the seat. He tried
to say something but his voice was
slurred. He had lost control of his move-
ments. I knew in an instant what it was,
for I had walked that path myself. It was
a stroke.

I jumped from the car, frantically waving my arms at the passing traffic. A
car full of old-age pensioners pulled
alongside.

"Is he drunk?" the driver said, peering through the window.

"Oh, no," I said, tears streaming down
my face. "He doesn't touch it. He's had
a stroke."

One of the men jumped out and helped
me push Rob to the other side of the
seat. He then drove us to a nearby phone

booth where I called Susan, Rob's wife. She met us at the Royal Adelaide Hospital where we waited anxious hours as the doctors worked with Rob. At last they reappeared. They had done all they could. Time would give us our answer.

I found a room at a nearby motel and collapsed into bed. My own heart was beating wildly, but I let my mind wander back in years to a scene that took place when Rob was eleven. He had been playing in the backyard. Jack and I were having tea when Rob came running into the kitchen.

"Dad, God just spoke to me and said He wanted me."

Jack reached out and rumpled Rod's hair. "Well, Rob, you go back to where you were, out under that old apple tree, and tell God you are quite ready."

A few minutes later Rob burst through the door back into the kitchen. "I told God what you told me," he grinned.

Jack smiled and nodded. Then seriously he added: "Look, Rob, write that down in your Bible, that on the 17th day of May, 1956, you accepted Jesus Christ as your Saviour. I'm asking you to do this because years from now the devil will come to you and try to convince you otherwise."

I lay on my bed, staring up at the ceiling. How clearly Rob's childish voice filled my mind—"Dad, God just spoke to me and said He wanted me."

"Dear Lord," I prayed silently, "Rob is not yet twenty-five. Surely You don't want him right now, do You?"

But God did want him—right then. Two days later he died. Only the inner presence of the Holy Spirit carried me through that ordeal, for had it not been for Him there would have been two funerals in that Presbyterian church, rather than one.

But the shock and grief proved to be too much for my tired heart. Susan and Caitlin visited us, and one night, just after Susan had taken the baby upstairs and put her to bed, I felt my lungs begin to tighten up. I was losing my breath. Standing in the hall between the dining room and the living room, I tried to call out to Susan. I could not. All I could do was slump against the wall, praying she would hurry down from upstairs. The world was rapidly closing in on me, like an evening fog that swirls in from the sea and smothers the ships in the harbor. I was backed into the corner of nothingness, strangling, gasping for air.

"I'm going to have an attack," I choked out as Susan came down the stairs. I staggered forward and pointed to the phone.

"Do you want me to call Dr. Etheridge?" Susan asked, alarmed.

I nodded. She dialed the doctor, but before she hung up, Jack walked in the back door. He knew, without asking, what was wrong. Hadn't he seen me, many times, in the same condition? I was standing against the wall, bent double from the waist, my lungs fighting for each breath.

Jack picked up the phone and called David Reekie. Moments later Dr. Etheridge rushed in. He listened to my chest with his stethoscope, took my blood pressure and then said, "Don't move.

I'm going to call an ambulance. You have an accumulation of fluid in your lung cavities. Edema. You're literally drowning and I've got to correct it immediately. I'm going for a hypodermic. I'll be back before the ambulance arrives."

Things were reeling by that time. I could hear some of the words; the rest drifted off into space. I knew Jack was pacing back and forth in front of the window. Bruce had left the room, weeping. The pain, raging through my chest, was worse than it had ever been. I was dying.

Then I was aware of David Reekie standing over me. He was praying.

Dr. Etheridge was back, almost pushing David out of the way as he stabbed the needle into my flesh . . . then the ambulance . . . and the flashing red lights outside the house again . . . and the swaying ride to the hospital . . . the weird wail of the siren . . . the mask over my face as the attendant gave me oxygen . . . and finally the intensive care unit of the hospital.

Once again I was saved by prayer. Within a week I was able to sit up in bed and listen while Dr. Etheridge stood over me, his voice steady but his face serious.

"Have you any idea how close we came to losing you?"

I nodded. "Jack has told me what you said," I said softly. "He says it was only the grace of God that I lived through it."

Dr. Etheridge nodded. "You can't go on like this. Your aorta valve is in critical condition. You must have an operation."

"No," I said solemnly. "Jack and I have prayed about it and we do not feel God wants me to have the surgery."

"You know," Dr. Etheridge said gravely, "you could reach the point of no return. If that comes, we'll have no choice but to do emergency surgery."

"And I have no choice but to survive on emergency prayer until God heals me," I said.

Reluctantly, Dr. Etheridge released me from the hospital with strict orders to stay at home. I kept remembering that touch of God in the tent meeting. Deep inside there was still hope, just a glimmer, that God might do it again.

6. I Need A Miracle

Months passed and it was only the lingering presence of little Caitlin that kept me in touch with reality. When Susan announced that she was going to remarry and move to Los Angeles, taking Caitlin with her, I thought the end had surely come. Tired and weary, the candle of hope flickered and almost went out.

It was Olive Reekie, I believe, who gave me my first copy of *I Believe in Miracles.* "That's what I need," I told Olive after I had pored through the book in one evening. "I need a miracle."

Olive had come by the house and we were sitting over a cup of tea. I had been in bed all morning, and was able to get out only for a few hours each afternoon.

"Pittsburgh is so far away," I said sadly. "If Miss Kuhlman would come even as close as California, I would jump a plane. I could then go see little Caitlin and be healed at the same time."

Olive blinked and half rose from her chair. "Morag, don't you know? Kathryn Kuhlman has meetings once a month in Los Angeles."

We talked on about many things, but I heard nothing. In my mind I was already buying tickets, packing suitcases and climbing aboard a Pan Am Airlines flight to Los Angeles. Surely this was a word from God—directly to me.

I had a shocking rash, like a bad case of eczema that covered great parts of my body. The Collins Street skin specialist, perhaps the leading dermatologist in Melbourne, had hospitalized me for it on several occasions. "You won't die from the rash," he had concluded, "but it will be with you forever. All we can do is ease the discomfort with an ointment."

Dr. Etheridge pointed out that the rash alone was bad enough to keep me home, not to mention my heart condition which was bound to be aggravated by the strain of flying ten thousand miles.

Oddly, despite the doctor's objections, Jack felt I should make the trip. "If God is speaking to you, dear," he said, "then I shall not stand in His way. I am believing with you that you will return to Australia healed."

Ten days later Bruce and I were winging our way to Los Angeles. Bruce had lost his job several months before. His blind eye and unpredictable blackouts, plus his overall condition made regular employment difficult. Jack felt that even though Bruce was now past thirty, he would be better off living with us where we could take care of him. I was glad to have him along, hoping he, too, might receive some kind of miracle.

Susan and her new husband, Steve, met our plane at the airport on Friday afternoon. We spent Saturday touring Beverly Hills with them. We stopped for lunch in a small restaurant off Wilshire Boulevard and after we ordered, Susan said, "Look in that window across the street. Isn't that a notice about this lady you've been speaking of, Kathryn Kuhlman?"

I turned and looked. There was a notice in the window of a shop saying, "Booking for Kathryn Kuhlman coaches." I could hardly wait to finish my meal.

The man in the shop explained that they had regular buses from this area of the city that went to the Kathryn Kuhlman Miracle Services. In fact, he said, there was a meeting scheduled for tomorrow afternoon at the Shrine Auditorium just south of the business district.

"Oh, can you reserve two seats for me on the coach?" I asked.

"I'm sorry," he said, shaking his head. "There is no more room. All our seats are taken."

"Look," I said, "just tell me how to get there. That's all I want to know."

"Say, where are you from?" the man said, noticing my accent.

"Australia."

"Australia! You mean you've come all the way from Australia just to attend a miracle service? Surely God will provide a way for you to get in, even though the coach is full."

I turned to Bruce. "Let's take a chance. The doors open at one o'clock so we had better get there early."

Early was the word. The next morning we were at the Shrine Auditorium at 5:45 a.m. There was already a crowd of people queued up around the front doors. It was going to be a long wait and I was concerned about my heart. Seldom on my feet for more than a few minutes at a time, now it seemed I would have to stand for almost seven hours. I turned to a woman standing beside me: "Does anybody ever die waiting to get into these meetings?"

She laughed. "I've been coming to the Miracle Services for some time. We always get here about sunup to get a place close to the door. Many of those who arrive early are desperately ill, but I've never known of anyone dying. The power of God surrounds this place on the day of the Miracle Service. He protects all those who come in faith."

That was reassuring, for I was already tired and weak. The woman, Orpha, introduced me to her friend June and we stood and talked. Others told me of the great services in the past and recounted many miracles they had seen. Just hearing these testimonies strengthened me.

All this friendliness amazed me, for I had heard that Yanks were self-centered materialists. The crowd outside the Shrine Auditorium was anything but that, however. It was more like a family and they recognized me simply as a sister from the other side of the world. None of us were strangers, just friends who had never met. Conversation flowed freely, as did ministry.

"Listen to this," I whispered to Bruce. Directly behind us was a man on crutches. He was telling the stranger next to him that he had driven down the night before from San Francisco. He had slept in his car in order to get in front of the line. The other man, a dentist from Los Angeles, reached out and laid his hands on the crippled man, praying that God would heal him during the service.

Such love—even among people who had never met before. This must be a place of God.

The hours passed like seconds. Suddenly the doors swung open and we were inside—seated in the second round of the balcony. It was like nothing I had ever experienced before. The crowd was warm, friendly, and most informal. Yet in spite of the friendly buzz of conversation, there was a holiness about the place. Church, I had been brought up to believe, should be a place where everyone sits like mummies, faces straight ahead, hands in lap, minds in neutral. But this giant auditorium, filled with more than seven thousand people, was vibrant with life.

The mighty choir was on stage, rehearsing. "It seems the choir should rehearse backstage and then come out and perform," I whispered to Bruce.

Still, as we sat and listened, I sensed something special about even the rehearsal. The silver-haired choir director, who I learned from the man next to me was actually one of America's most renowned musicians, would stop the choir in the middle of a song, make corrections, and then begin again. It was a typical choir rehearsal. Yet it wasn't typical. God was moving through those voices and I had to fight back the tears even as I listened. God was there.

From where we were sitting we could see the wheelchair section. All those in wheelchairs were allowed to come in early and occupy a reserved section in the auditorium. My heart reached out to a young boy, in his early teens, who was slumped in a wheelchair. He was so much like our little blind Johnny had been.

"Oh God," I prayed desperately, forgetting all about myself, "Johnny is in heaven with You. He never had the opportunity of being healed because we knew nothing of Your marvelous power. But, dear Father, this little boy has a chance. Please heal him."

Bruce reached over and clasped my hand in his. He didn't understand my tears; all he knew was something was wrong inside me. He reached out in love and compassion. I was glad I was not alone.

It never was clear to me when the meeting started. Most of our Australian churches have a formal call to worship, perhaps even a processional. But here in the big auditorium the love and praise just seemed to flow together and suddenly I was aware that Miss Kuhlman was on stage. The people were singing, the organ was booming, and the choir broke into a rendition of the song we had learned when Billy Graham came to Melbourne—"How Great Thou Art."

A spirit of praise seemed to sweep the mighty auditorium. The people rose, as one, and erupted in joyous acclamation of sound and harmony. All around me they were spontaneously coming to their feet, arms raised toward heaven, voices blending together in marvelous symphony. The entire room was filled with music. It swelled up from the main floor, vibrated off the walls and ceiling, and lifted my inner being to heights never before attained. I was worshiping. For the first time, perhaps in all my life, I was worshiping. I wanted to shout. I wanted to dance. I wanted to stretch my arms all the way through the elegant ceiling, through the clouds, all the way to the throne of heaven. Praise! What a wonderful word. Oh, how I praised *Him*!

7. All That Counted Was Jesus

I kept wanting to pull my eyes down and look at Miss Kuhlman. After all, I had come ten thousand miles to see her. But I could not look at her. I realized I had not come all the way from Australia to see Kathryn Kuhlman. I had come to see Jesus. To be touched by Him. It suddenly made no difference whether Kathryn Kuhlman was on stage or not. It made no difference whether she ever appeared. All that counted was Jesus—and we were His Body—prepared as a bride adorned for her husband— worshiping our coming King.

The singing changed to a song I had never heard.

He touched me—Oh, He touched me.
And oh, the joy that floods my soul.
Something happened and now I know
He touched me—and made me whole.

We sang it once, twice. It was as if the words had been a part of my soul all my life. I was swept up in the singing as the music soared all around me.

Slowly it died, until only the soft strains of the organ, barely heard, whispered through the room. Again I tried to lower my eyes to look at Miss Kuhlman, but could not. My hands were still outstretched toward heaven, my face up, my eyes shut. Softly, just above the sound of a breath, I heard Miss Kuhlman's voice. . .

"The Holy Spirit is here. He's here, just as He said He would be . . ."

The tears were washing down my cheeks as she continued. "There is power in the name of Jesus . . ."

All around me I heard that name, that matchless name, being whispered from muted lips of thousands. "Jesus . . . Jesus . . . Jesus."

"We know, Father," Miss Kuhlman's soft voice continued, "that miracles are already happening in this place. We promise to give You all the praise, all the glory. I know I am nothing . . . nothing . . . whatever happens in this place today is because of You . . ."

Then, growing out of a whisper and rising on the wings of praise, the choir and people were singing: "Alleluia! Alleluia!" But I could utter nothing as the music swept up from the main floor and swirled toward the heavens. All I could do was cry—openly, unashamedly, and murmur over and over, "Thank You, Jesus, thank You, Jesus."

As if the Holy Spirit knew we could stand no more of His glory, the atmosphere of the meeting changed. Miss Kuhlman became folksy, informal, and her soft laugh rippled over the congregation as she welcomed the people to the services. For the first time, I was able to look at her. She was not at all like I thought she would be. I had expected to see her with wings, and a halo, drifting three feet above the stage touching first this one and then that with a magic wand as the stars glittered around her head. Instead she seemed very human; in fact, almost Australian. She leaned on the speaker's stand with one elbow and welcomed the folks and made us feel so at home.

She introduced a group of ministers who were visiting—and the congregation roared its approval. Then she introduced a group from a nearby Catholic convent. A whole section of Catholic priests and nuns stood to their feet. There was another roar of recognition from the audience.

What is happening in the world? I wondered. Back home in Australia there are still areas where Catholics would not even be allowed to come into a Protestant meeting—yet here they were not only recognized, but applauded. Surely God is bringing His church together. I made a mental note to relate all this to my Presbyterian church when I returned.

Then Miss Kuhlman introduced a police captain from Houston, Texas. "Two years ago," she said, "Captain John LeVrier was dying of cancer. Entire portions of his body had been eaten away. He flew to Los Angeles as a last resort. Look at him now."

The crowd was on its feet applauding as the robust police officer made his way to the microphone. I sat, entranced, as he told how the doctors had given him up. A Baptist deacon, he knew nothing about the healing power of God until he saw Miss Kuhlman on television and then read her books. Believing that God could heal him, he flew to Los Angeles to attend a Miracle Service. And God did heal him. Instantly. He has since been filled with the Holy Spirit and is spending much of his time traveling around the nation testifying to the power of God.

That's the secret, I thought. *Once you are healed you must be willing to testify. For if you don't claim it, it will never be yours.* I thought back to the tent meeting in Melbourne, when I was so sure God had touched me. Yet I had been ashamed to testify to the doctor, afraid he would laugh at me.

"If you'll give me one more chance,

Lord," I promised, "I'll tell the world."

"There is a beautiful presence of the Holy Spirit here this afternoon," Miss Kuhlman was saying. "The same Holy Spirit that fell upon those early believers at Pentecost is here today."

A sacred, holy stillness descended upon the meeting. Like the moaning of the night wind as it vanishes into the stillness, so all sound—even, it seemed, the breathing of the people—faded away into the hush of reverence.

"There is a child being healed," she whispered. "He's in this section." She gestured to her left at the wheelchair section. My eyes followed the direction of her extended arm and I saw that young boy, that crippled, twisted young boy, rising out of his wheelchair.

A gasp went up from the audience. All over the auditorium people were rising to their feet, stretching their necks to see. The boy and his mother were out in the aisle, walking forward. A cheer, that started as a low rumble, grew with intensity and swept through the crowd.

The boy's steps seemed to grow stronger as he moved down the aisle. Miss Kuhlman met him at the front edge of the platform and escorted him to the microphone. Holy pandemonium broke loose in the auditorium as the people roared with joy.

"This applause is not for me," Miss Kuhlman said to the young lad, "nor is it even for you. These people are applauding Jesus."

After questioning the boy and even having one of the doctors on the platform step out and examine him, Miss Kuhlman reached out to pray for him. Even before she uttered her first word, the boy crumpled to the floor.

My heart sank. *Oh no, it wasn't real. It was all emotion. He tried and got as far as the platform, but now he's fallen to the floor. How awful!*

But no one else seemed alarmed. Miss Kuhlman was standing on stage, her hands raised, praising the Lord. The ushers, the members of the choir—all were standing around looking at the boy and thanking God. One of the men helped the boy to his feet. He wasn't staggering.

His legs were firm and strong.

"What happened?" I asked the man beside me, who had been to the meetings many times before.

"He went down under the power," he said.

"Under the power? What a strange phrase."

"Not so strange," the man whispered as the young boy left the stage with his mother. "It happens all the time when Miss Kuhlman prays for people. She says she doesn't understand it, and neither does anyone else. It's the same thing that happened in the Bible when people came face to face with the power of God, and fell to the ground."

It was too much to comprehend.

There was another healing in the wheelchair section. A lady, whom I had noticed outside the building, had come forward. While in the wheelchair she had to breathe from an oxygen tank, which was attached to the chair. Now she was coming across the stage, pushing the wheelchair in front of her—the oxygen tank hanging uselessly to the frame. Behind her was a great line of other people who had been healed and were coming to the stage to testify.

8. "Oh, Thank God, It's Me!"

I lost track of time as one after another the people came forward. It was so much different from the tent meeting I had attended in Melbourne. There they had brought the sick forward and the evangelist had prayed for them. Here the people came forward *after* they were healed. Miss Kuhlman prayed for no one ✗ to be healed. In fact, several times that afternoon she definitely said she was not a healer. She had no power herself, she insisted. All she did was conduct the service and God did the healing. "If the

Holy Spirit were not here," she said, "then even though I were here, and the choir sang and the musicians played— there would be no healing. For God alone heals—not man."

The meeting was drawing to a close. Neither Bruce nor I had evidenced any personal healing, but we had been blessed beyond all expectation. An announcement was made for a future meeting in December, less than a month away. I knew we should remain in the States in order to return once more.

Susan and Steve found us a beautiful room in Encinitas, down the coast from Los Angeles, where we could relax and enjoy being in this beautiful section of America. Three days later Bruce and I had returned to the room after breakfast. I was sitting quietly in a chair near the window reading my Bible when Bruce interrupted me.

"Mum, show me your hands."

"What's all this?" I answered, laying aside my Bible.

"Your hands," Bruce insisted. "Look at them."

I gasped. The rash was gone. How long it had been gone I had no idea. Perhaps it had disappeared during the night. Perhaps it had been while I was reading my Bible. But it was gone.

I hurried into the bathroom and examined other parts of my body. The ugly, red rash, which had become so much a part of me that I had forgotten about it, had disappeared. Not a trace was left. The rest of the day, indeed for many days thereafter, I spent the majority of my time praising God for this miraculous deliverance. Surely, I felt, it was the first sign that God intended to heal my heart also.

I placed an overseas telephone call to Jack. He rejoiced with me and encouraged me to stay on as long as I wanted. He missed me terribly, he said, but felt strongly that God was going to heal me. He'd rather have me gone for a month, he said, than for a lifetime.

We moved back up to Los Angeles and returned to the Shrine Auditorium for the December meeting. Once again, arriving before six o'clock in the morning,

I found my new friends, Orpha and June, in the queue. The front doors swung open promptly at one o'clock and as before we were swallowed up in the moving mass of human bodies which flowed into the auditorium like floodwaters down a dry riverbed.

As before I was caught up in the presence of the Holy Spirit which seemed to permeate every corner of that great building. The meeting had scarcely started when Miss Kuhlman, in her warm, informal manner, began polling the people in the audience to see where they were from.

"How many here from Kansas?" A score of people stood to their feet. "How about Texas?" A dozen others stood. "Just call out where you are from," Miss Kuhlman laughed. "I'll bet every state is represented, plus many foreign countries."

My heart was beating rapidly as people called out their home states. *Should I shout out AUSTRALIA?* I wondered. Then, even before I had a chance to say anything, I heard something else. It was a rushing, gushing sound of wind whirling through the auditorium.

I looked up, expecting to see the huge drape which covers the ceiling, billowing in the wind. Nothing was moving. I looked at the stage; perhaps it was coming from there. The drapes were hanging motionless. No one else seemed to notice it.

I turned to Bruce. "Do you hear it?" I said.

"Hear what, Mum?" he asked.

Am I losing my mind, hearing sounds that aren't there? I wondered. I turned to Orpha who was sitting on the other side. "Can you hear that noise?"

She shrugged and said, "What noise?"

"It's a rushing noise, like the sound of the wind."

Orpha looked deep into my face. "Do you still hear it?" she asked.

"Yes, it's all through the building."

Orpha's lips grew white and she said with shaking voice. "It's the Holy Spirit. It's your healing. Let's join hands and pray."

Miss Kuhlman was still taking a poll

of the states as Orpha, June, Bruce and I joined hands down the row and began to pray. I felt a wonderful peace. At the same time there was a pumping sensation throbbing in my chest. I closed my eyes and could visualize the blood, long held in check beyond that blocked valve, now surging through the healed organ, pulsating out into my lungs and through my body. Along with it came an exquisite inner calm.

I relaxed in my seat and heard nothing for the next twenty minutes. It was as though I had dropped off to sleep, although Orpha later suggested I was really "under the power."

Then, as the voice of Jesus called dead Lazarus to rise and come forth from the tomb, I heard Miss Kuhlman's voice, rousing me from my reverie.

"There is someone in the center section, a dozen or so rows back, who has received a healing for a blockage in the chest—perhaps a blockage to the heart."

I was on my feet, waving my arms. "It's me!" I shouted. "Oh, thank God, it's me!"

Gone was my Scottish reserve, my Presbyterian dignity. Gone was the fear of ridicule, the shame of public opinion. I had denied Him once before; I would never do it again—even if I were laughed at or nailed to a cross.

I dived for the aisle, tromping on people's feet, banging against their knees as they tried to move aside for me to get out. Behind me I could hear Bruce. "Mum, Mum, I can see colors out of my blind eye. My sight is returning!"

I reached back, grabbed his hand and pulled him along with me. We barged out of the row of seats and into the aisle. An usher met us and tried to block our way.

"What have we here?" he said kindly, determined not to let me get to the platform unless my healing was genuine.

I was unable to reply, unable to articulate. I guess my Australian accent was bad enough without having all my words jumbled together in excitement.

"It's me," I said over and over. "I am the one Kathryn Kuhlman was talking about. I'm healed."

I finally made him understand that I had received healing of my heart. Even as I stood there in the aisle, it was becoming more and more evident. The old tiredness, which I had lived with for twenty years was gone. I could feel my blood flowing freely through my body. I could breathe, long deep gasps of air all the way down to the bottom of my lungs. And the rattle in my heart, that awful rickety sound which used to wake me at night, was gone. I was healed.

The usher escorted me to the stage where a medical doctor pulled me aside for a few minutes and talked to me. He asked question after question, but like the usher, had a difficult time understanding me.

"Have you a husband?" he finally asked.

"Yes, back in Australia."

"Do you mean you came all the way from Australia to America to be healed?"

"On a wing and a prayer," I laughed.

I had almost forgotten about Bruce who was standing behind me. I grabbed his

hand and pulled him toward Miss Kuhlman. The doctor was telling her something about my aorta valve . . . Australia
. . . Bruce . . . and suddenly I was on my
back on the floor. For a moment I had
a vision of Elijah, ascending to heaven
in a whirlwind, and then it was like the
emerald South Pacific at dawn, stretching for limitless miles beyond the hori-
zon, calm and glassy, with only a slight
ripple on the beach.

Someone helped me to my feet and
I saw Miss Kuhlman's face in front of
me, smiling. She reached out again and
I slipped back into the serenity of that
ocean of peace.

Strong arms lifted me back to me feet.
I tried to speak to Miss Kuhlman, but
I felt myself once again being im-
mersed—slipping into the gentle tide of
the Holy Spirit.

"Don't touch her," I heard Miss Kuhlman's soft voice from some place far
away. "That's the power of God."

I do not know how long I remained
on the platform, but some minutes later
I was aware that two men were helping

me to my feet. Bruce was in front of me, as we went down the steps to the main floor. He had removed his glasses and his face was wet with tears. Even though he could not see clearly out of his blind eye, it was miracle enough for him that he could see colors and shapes.

To this day I cannot remember how we got back to our room in downtown Los Angeles. I remember stepping off the bus about a block away from the Oasis Motel and feeling so joyful that I began to skip and sing. "Oh, God is good, oh, God is good, praise the Lord, for the Lord is good."

"Shush, Mum, shush," Bruce said, embarrassed. "There are people looking."

Indeed there were. People in a booth alongside the street were staring at me. People in their cars, waiting for a traffic light, were looking. It meant nothing. I knew I would never again be ashamed of the power of God.

"Who cares?" I laughed at Bruce. "Come, let's run and sing all the way to the room."

I wanted to call Jack in Australia, but I knew he was in Sydney that day on a business trip. It made no difference, we were scheduled to leave early the next morning on a flight back to Melbourne and he would meet us at the airport. I could surprise him then.

We said our good-bys to Caitlin and her parents. This time, however, it was not as before. No longer was she the center of my life, my tie with reality. With Jesus at the center of my life, Caitlin, as much as I loved her, was simply another of God's precious children. Not only had God replaced my aorta valve, He had healed my broken heart. Little Johnny's death, Rob's death, Bruce's continued affliction—all were in God's hand. It is God who rules the universe, who touches each life, who lets His rain fall on the just and the unjust. I knew I would return home and smother Jack with my love—a love I had not been able to give for years because of my weariness and pain. I would stand in our Presbyterian church at the invitation of the minister and testify for all to hear that I had been healed by the power of the Holy Spirit.

I settled in my seat on the Pan Am

747. The captain announced we would be flying through a hurricane and warned all the passengers to buckle in tight and not be afraid. I smiled, leaned back, and prepared to go to sleep. Nothing frightened me any more. I was whole.

It was December, the end of autumn in America. In twenty hours we would fly into summer in Australia. But geography made no difference to me. I did not have to return to the "land down under" to find summer in December—it had already begun in my heart.

The year's at the spring
And the day's at the morn . . .
God's in his heaven—
All's right with the world.

Epilogue

Following her return to Australia, Mrs. McDougall's first public encounter came the following Sunday morning with her minister and his wife, Dr. and Mrs. Gordon Powell. Mrs. McDougall had just entered the beautiful sanctuary of her Presbyterian church when Mrs. Powell grabbed her arm, pulled her to one side, and whispered, "My, you're looking well. Jack said you had been on a holiday to the States. It must have done you a world of good."

Morag grinned and replied, "I've been

healed by the power of the Holy Spirit.'' She then proceeded to tell the minister's wife the entire story. Dr. Gordon Powell is among the Presbyterian ministers in Australia who teach spiritual healing and pray for the sick at the Sunday night service. Interested, the Powells invited the McDougalls to the manse in order to hear Morag's full testimony.

Several months later, Dr. Powell asked Mrs. McDougall to speak during a Sunday evening service, testifying of her healing. Later she shared her testimony over his nationwide radio broadcast.

Mrs. McDougall's second encounter was with Dr. Maurice Etheridge. Dr. Etheridge had been on a long Christmas holiday when she returned, so it was the first of February before he was able to examine her.

"How was the trip?" he inquired as Mrs. McDougall prepared for her examination in his office.

"Fine," Morag answered, determined not to say anything until the doctor confirmed her healing.

"Show me your hands," he said. The

rash was gone and the doctor made notes in his records.

Next he took her blood pressure. It was normal. He made more notes.

Her lungs were perfect also. "You should have stayed in America," Dr. Etheridge murmured as he made additional notes.

Biting her tongue, Mrs. McDougall said nothing.

Asking her to sit on the examination table, Dr. Etheridge began a thorough examination with his stethoscope. Morag was praying silently. "Oh, Lord, You know I'm healed. I know I'm healed. Let the doctor find it out also."

"Amazing," Dr. Etheridge said as he listened, first to her chest and then to her back. "Amazing. The rattle is no longer there."

Folding his stethoscope and putting it in his pocket, he sat down at his desk and began making final notations on Morag's file. Finishing his writing, he leaned back in his chair and said, "Now, tell me what *really* happened in America."

For a second, for a fleeting second,

there was a temptation to say nothing. But she had gone too far already. Taking a deep breath Morag said, "Well, Doctor, medical science is wonderful, but you do believe God can heal, don't you?"

Dr. Etheridge smiled slightly and drummed his fingers on the top of his desk. "If God ever heals anybody, I believe He would heal you."

That opened the door and Morag poured out her testimony. She told him the entire story: the visit to the Miracle Service, even the sensation of power and peace as she fell to the floor three times at the Shrine Auditorium.

Dr. Etheridge listened patiently. Then donning his leather apron and heavy gloves, took four X-ray pictures of her heart and lungs. All were negative. She was healed. He closed his file and replaced it in his drawer.

"You are a remarkably well woman," he said.

As the word spread through the "land down under" that Morag McDougall had been given a new heart, she ran into critics. "Why did you have to go to

America? Don't you believe God can heal here also?" one woman asked.

"I do not know why the Ethiopian had to wait until he was in the desert to find out about Jesus, when God could have told him while he was visiting in Jerusalem," Morag answered. "Nor why God waited until Saul of Tarsus was on the road to Damascus to speak to him, rather than in his home town. Nor why I had to go ten thousand miles for a miracle. All that is God's business. You may question Him if you wish—I shall simply praise Him."

Another said, "We do not doubt that God can heal. But why do you insist on talking about it all the time?"

Morag is not defensive. Neither is she ashamed. Her answer, she says, is found in a verse of Scripture which has taken on special meaning since her healing. *"Behold, I have set before thee an open door, and no man can shut it:* *for thou hast a little strength, and hast kept my word, and hast not denied my name"* (Rev. 3:8).